The **INSIDE GUIDE**

ROBOTICS

Robots in

Defense

By Sadie Silva

Cavendish Square

New York

Published in 2022 by Cavendish Square Publishing, LLC
243 5th Avenue, Suite 136, New York, NY 10016

Website: cavendishsq.com

This publication represents the opinions and views of the author based on his or her personal experience, knowledge, and research. The information in this book serves as a general guide only. The author and publisher have used their best efforts in preparing this book and disclaim liability rising directly or indirectly from the use and application of this book.

Portions of this work were originally authored by Daniel R. Faust and published as *Military and Police Robots (Robots and Robotics)*. All new material this edition authored by Sadie Silva.

All websites were available and accurate when this book was sent to press.

Library of Congress Cataloging-in-Publication Data

Names: Silva, Sadie, author.
Title: Robots in defense / Sadie Silva.
Description: New York : Cavendish Square Publishing, [2022] | Series: The inside guide: robotics | Includes index.
Identifiers: LCCN 2020024417 | ISBN 9781502660640 (library binding) | ISBN 9781502660626 (paperback) | ISBN 9781502660633 (set) | ISBN 9781502660657 (ebook)
Subjects: LCSH: Military robots–Juvenile literature. | Robotics–Military applications–Juvenile literature.
Classification: LCC UG450 .S42 2022 | DDC 623–dc23
LC record available at https://lccn.loc.gov/2020024417

Editor: Caitie McAneney
Copyeditor: Jill Keppeler
Designer: Deanna Paternostro

The photographs in this book are used by permission and through the courtesy of: Cover Justin Sullivan/Getty Images News/Getty Images; p. 4 Digital Storm/Shutterstock.com; p. 6 (top) thieury/Shutterstock.com; p. 6 (bottom) Sundry Photography/Shutterstock.com; p. 7 Collection 68/Alamy Stock Photo; p. 8 Isaac Brekken/Getty Images News/Getty Images; p. 9 Paul Taggart/Bloomberg via Getty Images; p. 10 Stocktrek Images/Stocktrek Images/Getty Images; p. 12 Chip Somodevilla/Getty Images News/Getty Images; p. 13 Christian Charisius/picture alliance via Getty Images; p. 14 U.S. Navy photo by John F. Williams; pp. 15, 27 (top) Kiyoshi Ota/Bloomberg via Getty Images; p. 16 Andrew Renneisen/Getty Images News/Getty Images; p. 18 (top) Photoshot/Hulton Archive/Getty Images; p. 18 (bottom) Leoty X/Andia/Universal Images Group via Getty Images; p. 19 Nigel Roddis /Getty Images News/Getty Images; p. 20 Saul Loeb/AFP via Getty Images; p. 21 Zein Al-Rifai/AFP via Getty Images; p. 22 Jonathan Nackstrand/AFP via Getty Images; p. 24 Michael Fitzsimmons/Alamy Stock Photo; p. 26 PJF Military Collection/Alamy Stock Photo; p. 27 (bottom) WENN Rights Ltd/Alamy Stock Photo; p. 28 (top) Alberto Pizzoli/AFP via Getty Images; p. 28 (bottom) Joe Raedle/Getty Images News/Getty Images; p. 29 (top) Miguel Medina/AFP via Getty Images; p. 29 (bottom) Ben Birchall/PA Images via Getty Images.

Some of the images in this book illustrate individuals who are models. The depictions do not imply actual situations or events.

CPSIA compliance information: Batch #CS22CSQ: For further information contact Cavendish Square Publishing LLC, New York, New York, at 1-877-980-4450.

Printed in the United States of America

Find us on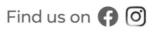

CONTENTS

Because they can work without getting tired and can keep humans out of unsafe situations, robots are useful for military and police work.

ROBOTS ON A MISSION

Robots perform amazing tasks, including flying and making products in factories. Some are even built for the battlefield. Militaries and law enforcement agencies around the world use robots to handle dangerous defense situations alongside officers and soldiers.

Robots at the Ready

Military and law enforcement robots are built for specific jobs. Some are built to work on the ground, while others are aerial, which means they operate in the air. Most robots—from factory robots to drones—share the same basic components, or parts, including sensors, a frame, actuators, effectors, and a controller.

Fast Fact

Drones are unmanned aircraft usually guided by a person on the ground. These flying robots are used for military operations, search-and-rescue operations, and even important deliveries.

Sensors gather information about a robot's surroundings. Some robots have cameras and microphones that act like eyes and ears. Some have special sensors that allow them to detect temperature, air pressure, and **radiation** levels, as well as changes to Earth's magnetic field.

Thermal imaging allows drones to sense differences in heat across an area.

Effectors and actuators are a robot's moving parts. Effectors interact directly with the robot's surroundings. They allow a robot to perform specific tasks, such as lifting and moving objects. Actuators are the motors that power the effectors. They also power the parts that make a robot move, such as wheels, treads, and propellers.

The controller is the robot's "brain," moving some robots according to a series of preprogrammed, or set, actions. Other robots are controlled remotely, or by a person using a separate controller.

Robots in Military History

Military robots have changed throughout the years. During World War I (1914–1918), the United States developed an unmanned

This police officer is holding a flight controller that remotely controls a drone.

aerial torpedo, or bomb, called the Kettering Bug. This flying bomb could hit a target that was miles away. During World War II (1939–1945), the German army used the remote-controlled Goliath vehicle. It could carry more than 130 pounds (59 kilograms) of explosives. The Goliath was used against tanks, bridges, buildings, and enemy soldiers.

During the same war, the Soviet Union created remote-controlled unmanned tanks called teletanks, which had flamethrowers, machine guns, and sometimes timed bombs. The Goliath vehicles and teletanks were able to get close to the enemy with less risk to the people who controlled them.

The Vietnam War (1954–1975) saw more advancements to drone (also called UAV, or unmanned aerial vehicle) warfare. Drones made it possible to fly over enemy territory and gather **intelligence** without risking the lives of human pilots.

Drones such as this one were used for reconnaissance, or gathering information, during the Vietnam War.

In the 21st century, the U.S. military **deployed** new technology—the Predator UAV—to fight the "War on Terror." The Predator fired its first missile in combat on October 7, 2001, beginning a shift in aerial military combat from manned aircraft to remote-piloted aircraft.

Today's Technology

Today, defense robots are used for **surveillance**, reconnaissance, bomb location and removal, and armed combat. Engineers are developing new UGVs, such as the Gladiator Tactical UGV, which can monitor areas and fire at enemies when necessary. UAVs such as the Predator B can find enemies and strike on command.

Engineers with government agencies and private labs are improving robotics technology each year. In the right hands, robotics technology can ensure that military and law enforcement operations save as many lives as possible.

The Predator B (also known as the MQ-9 Reaper) can fly more than 50,000 feet (15,240 meters) above ground at nearly 150 miles (241 kilometers) per hour for 27 hours. It can carry a 500 percent greater **payload** than the Predator.

DARPA

The United States Department of Defense has an agency dedicated to developing new military technology. This agency is called DARPA, which stands for Defense Advanced Research Projects Agency. The agency was a response to foreign competition in technology.

DARPA was developed in 1958 when the Soviet Union launched Sputnik, the first man-made **satellite**. DARPA is responsible for the development of new and emerging defense technologies. The agency's scientific breakthroughs in the areas of medicine, robotics, and computer science are useful to both the military and the public. This agency is working with top engineers to develop future military robotics technology, including wearable robotic suits for soldiers and robot insect spies.

This tiny hummingbird robot was developed with help from DARPA to be an undercover spy.

This TALON robot is shown here disposing of an unexploded mortar, or explosive device.

Robots can do some of the most dangerous, or unsafe, jobs on Earth and in space. From bomb disposal bots to battlefield medics, robots can take over dangerous defense missions and save the day.

Disposing of Danger

Special military robots such as the MARCbot and TALON robot are used to locate, disarm, or dispose of explosives and other **hazardous** materials, or hazmat. Bomb disposal robots come in different shapes and sizes, but they have many features in common.

The MARCbot was one of the most common robots used to inspect suspicious objects during U.S. military missions during the Iraq War (2003–2011). About the size of a big remote-controlled car, the MARCbot is small enough to look under furniture and vehicles. Lights, cameras, and special sensors help the robot locate mines, hazardous chemicals, and improvised explosive devices (IEDs). IEDs hurt and killed thousands of people in Iraq.

Fast Fact

The term "MARCbot" stands for Multi-Function Agile Remote Control Robot. It was developed through a partnership with the U.S. space agency NASA.

Arms with gripper claws allow these kinds of robots to move explosives and other dangerous objects away from soldiers and **civilians**. The robots are controlled remotely by a soldier at a safe distance away.

Robots Save the Day!

Soldiers hurt in combat could die on a battlefield if a medical professional, or medic, isn't around to save them. However, that puts medics at risk in war zones. Could robots be the answer to this problem?

This remote-controlled MARCbot has a video camera to help its human controllers inspect dangerous areas.

The U.S. Army is developing new robots for medical uses. Engineers hope to develop robots that can help soldiers who are in hard-to-reach and unsafe areas. The robots may be able to help stop a soldier's bleeding, tend to burns, and assist with brain injuries.

In the future, unmanned ambulances may rescue these soldiers from unsafe situations. Robot medics could also deliver medical supplies to soldiers in enemy territory. These robot medics could mean the difference between life and death for a wounded soldier or civilian.

Built for Disaster

Sometimes law enforcement and military personnel are needed in the middle of a disaster such as a horrible hurricane or blazing wildfire. New technology can often be helpful in these cases.

Police departments, fire departments, and other emergency services are using robots to assist their efforts after accidents and natural disasters. After a natural disaster such as an earthquake or hurricane, survivors may be trapped. Unmanned robot boats can bring stranded people to safety. Drones can help

The da Vinci Xi surgical system allows a surgeon to operate remotely on a patient by guiding robotic arms.

SAFFIR

In 2015, the U.S. Navy unveiled a humanlike firefighting robot called SAFFiR (Shipboard Autonomous Firefighting Robot). Fires on ships are one of the greatest dangers to sailors, military or civilian. SAFFiR is built with materials that are **resistant** to fire and is shaped like a human so it can walk easily through the ship. It has special sensors that allow it to detect fires and see through smoke. SAFFiR's job is to go onto a ship and try to put out the flames. It's built for **maneuvering** in narrow ship passages, keeping its balance on choppy seas, and releasing firefighting materials.

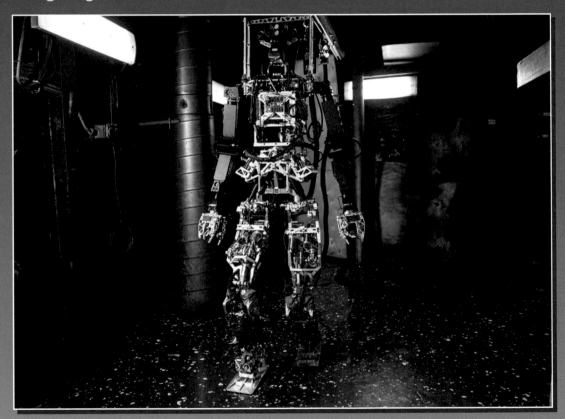

In this 2014 photograph, SAFFiR is tested aboard a military ship.

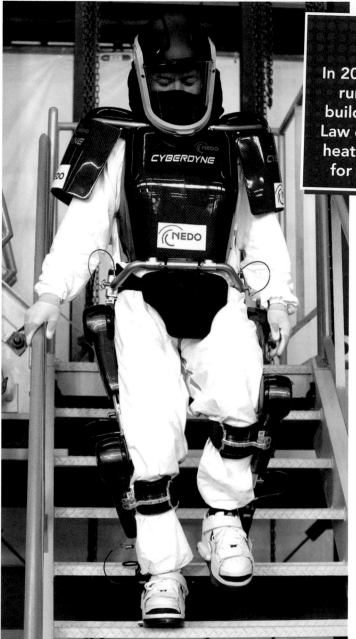

Engineers are developing robotic suits (such as the one shown here) that can help with disaster relief, rescue, and cleanup.

people judge damage and find survivors among wreckage. Robots can deliver water, medicine, and supplies to people waiting to be rescued. The National Oceanic and Atmospheric Administration (NOAA) has also sent unmanned robots into the ocean to collect data that can help it forecast deadly hurricanes before they happen.

Surveillance drones can help
military and law enforcement
officials patrol and study an area.

Some robots are built to be spies that work with **stealth** and speed. They can search an area for people who are hurt or lost or for enemies in dangerous areas. They can find out information in dangerous situations so that military officials can plan safer missions.

Robot Reconnaissance

Reconnaissance is important to military operations. It means gathering information about a region to locate an enemy or create a plan. Surveillance is important too. In these situations, flying robots such as drones can be the perfect fit for the job.

Fast Fact

Remote-controlled UAVs have been used for decades. The AQM-34 Ryan Firebee was used over Southeast Asia in the Vietnam War, becoming an important surveillance tool.

Drones can be launched over enemy territory, where they can remain for hours or even days, providing full-color, real-time video of enemy troops. Military drones can be equipped with advanced cameras, video cameras, and thermal-imaging sensors. These aircraft provide troops with valuable information so they can plan their next move.

The Ryan Firebee was one of the first jet-powered drones. After completing a mission, the Firebee would let out a parachute, or large cloth, and drop into a safe area.

The military drones of tomorrow may not only be much more advanced, but also much smaller. DARPA is even working on technology to create cyborg—half-alive, half-machine—insects, which humans could control in flight to obtain important information in a covert, or secret, way.

Robot Search Parties

Reconnaissance and surveillance drones aren't only important in times of war and disaster. They're also important for helping authorities find people who are lost or hiding.

Surveillance information provided by drones can save the lives of military and law enforcement officers during dangerous times, such as **pandemics**. This photograph shows French police officers using drones during the COVID-19 pandemic.

INSECT CYBORGS

DARPA has been trying to create tiny drones called micro air vehicles (MAVs) since the 1940s. However, engineers realized that insects and small flying mammals are already some of the best MAVs around. Engineers and scientists began exploring the idea of developing HI-MEMs, or Hybrid Insect Micro-Electro-Mechanical systems. Scientists would insert mechanical parts into baby bugs to make them half-insect and half-machine—insect cyborgs. Modifying the insect's body would let a person control its behavior and capture images from the sky. These cyborg insects could be important in reconnaissance and surveillance missions because no one would suspect them, and they could fit into small spaces.

The military is developing some smaller UAVs, like this Black Hornet Nano helicopter.

Pilots such as this one can fly military UAVs over tropical storms and hurricanes to keep an eye on changing weather conditions, which can help officials save lives.

Flying robots can be faster and more successful than human search parties when someone is lost in the wilderness. A single drone can search several miles in a matter of minutes, while it would take a human search party several hours. Unlike people, drones can search day and night. They can even see through clouds, rain, and fog.

Drones can also be used to help police search for suspected criminals. **Infrared** and low-light cameras can help police identify their targets at night or in bad weather. Drones can fly over a neighborhood and determine which buildings are occupied

Fast Fact

In 2019, Chinese law enforcement used a drone to find an escaped criminal who had been on the run for 17 years. The drone found the criminal in a cave in the mountains.

by sensing the heat given off by a human body. These crime-fighting drones help keep law enforcement officers safe.

Urban Robot Spies

Robots can be designed to search and fight in many different kinds of environments. In recent years, the U.S. military has developed robots that can be used for reconnaissance and surveillance in tightly packed city spaces.

To help soldiers and law enforcement in city areas, drones can fly overhead and map out streets and buildings. Small UGVs or UAVs can be sent into areas ahead of soldiers to locate traps and enemy fighters. These robots can peek around corners, into windows, or even inside sewer pipes. Larger robots can break down doors, walls, and other obstacles, as well as carry additional equipment and supplies. These robots are masters of searching and spying in close quarters. In the near future, city-use robots might be controlled remotely by users wearing robot-paired **virtual reality** headsets and "hand-pose detection gloves," allowing them guide the robot more easily.

Fighting a war in a city landscape poses its own set of obstacles, including buildings, alleys, and the increased presence of civilians.

Fast Fact

The U.S. Army is trying to develop robots for subterranean, or underground, warfare. The robots could map, navigate, and help fight against enemies in underground tunnels.

One of the most advanced UAVs outside of the U.S. military is the Heron TP, used by the Israel Defense Forces. It can fly for more than 30 hours and can carry guided bombs and air-to-ground missiles.

ROBOTS IN COMBAT

Bomb disposal, dangerous rescue missions, reconnaissance, and surveillance are important jobs in the fight against enemies. However, sometimes robots are called to more direct action—combat.

Military UCAVs

Unmanned combat aerial vehicles (UCAVs) are important players in military defense today. Before UCAVs were invented, all aerial combat planes had to be flown directly by pilots, which can be very risky. The United States—as well as nations such as Turkey, China, United Arab Emirates, United Kingdom, and Israel—has developed advanced UCAVs in recent years.

Fast Fact

Many names exist for unmanned aircraft. A UAV (unmanned aerial vehicle) is a part of a UAS (unmanned aircraft system), which also includes a remote pilot. RPA (remotely piloted aircraft) is also a common term.

Combat drones may carry missiles and bombs as well as the targeting computers needed to fire them. Because they need to carry heavy weapons, combat drones are usually fairly large—almost as large as regular aircraft. Predator

Air Force MQ-9 Reaper drone

There are questions about the ethics of using combat drones because they sometimes miss their targets and kill civilians.

drones changed military history in the early 2000s when they began airstrikes. Today, newer UCAVs such as the Predator B (MQ-9 Reaper) and Predator C Avenger can fly faster and higher and can carry much greater payloads. Human pilots still have to give the drones direction during the missions, but they are safe while the drone goes into combat.

Military UGVs

UGVs also operate without a human controller on board. Operated by handheld controller or a command console, UGVs travel over the ground into dangerous territory, and some are equipped for combat.

DEFENSE SWARMS

Someday, robot swarms—or teams—might take part in military operations. These groups of **autonomous** UAVs and UGVs would work together to launch an attack or defend against an attacker. These defense swarms first need to be able to "think" like human soldiers and use "swarm intelligence," like a group of ants working together. In 2020, DARPA gave money to the University at Buffalo to study the eye movements and brain waves of gamers. They want to use the data collected to develop artificial intelligence for robot swarms. Robot swarms could be nearly impossible to defend against.

A Timeline of UAVs in the Military

1910s:	The first simple UAVs are developed and tested for military use.
1940s:	Germany uses the V-1 UAV, which is able to drop bombs, leading to future U.S. UAV development programs.
1950s and 1960s:	The U.S. military uses the Ryan Firebee UAV for surveillance during the Vietnam War.
1980s:	The Israeli Air Force begins developing advanced versions of UAVs, inspiring the U.S. military in their design.
2001:	The United States launches the first armed drone strikes. UAVs such as the MQ-1 Predator, MQ-9 Reaper (Predator B), and RQ-4 Global Hawk are deployed in Afghanistan and the Middle East.
2013:	British troops begin using the Black Hornet Nano helicopter for surveillance.
2019:	The U.S. Air Force demonstrates a new stealth UAV called the XQ-58A Valkyrie.

The U.S. military first started using TALON robots in 2001. These lightweight, unmanned robots can be used in military operations as well as law enforcement and first responder missions. The TALON has sensors to detect gas, chemicals, radiation, and temperature levels, as well as a microphone and a robotic arm.

The first weaponized UGV was an adaptation of the TALON robot called SWORDS, or Special Weapons Observation Reconnaissance Detection System. It could carry machine guns, automatic rifles, grenade launchers, or flamethrowers.

Robo-Soldiers of the Future!

Will humanoid robots fight the wars of tomorrow? We likely have a long way to go, and there are many ethical questions around the idea of robots fighting our battles for us. Many people worry about developing autonomous defense robots.

Fast Fact

The Gladiator Tactical UGV is a mobile robotic system armed with automatic weapons that was in development for many years, but it hasn't been widely used yet.

One of the most humanoid, or humanlike, robots so far is the Atlas robot, which was developed by Boston Dynamics for search and rescue.

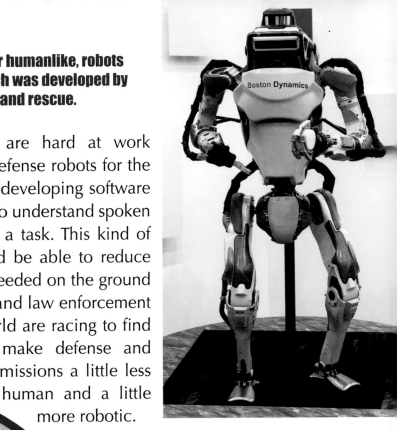

However, engineers are hard at work creating smarter, faster defense robots for the future. The U.S. Army is developing software that would allow robots to understand spoken instructions to carry out a task. This kind of "intelligent" robot would be able to reduce the number of soldiers needed on the ground for a mission. Militaries and law enforcement agencies around the world are racing to find technologies that will make defense and rescue missions a little less human and a little more robotic.

Fast Fact

Spot, a robot dog, was employed to help officials in Singapore enforce social distancing during the COVID-19 pandemic in 2020.

Robot dogs might be a thing of the future! BigDog was a robot developed to carry supplies, but it was too loud to work in combat situations.

THINK ABOUT IT!

1. In the future, drones will probably be used more often to help out in natural disaster situations. In which situations do you think they'd be helpful?

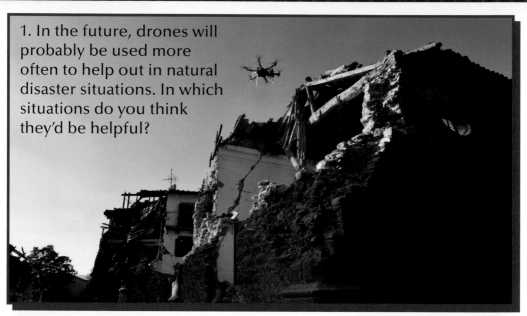

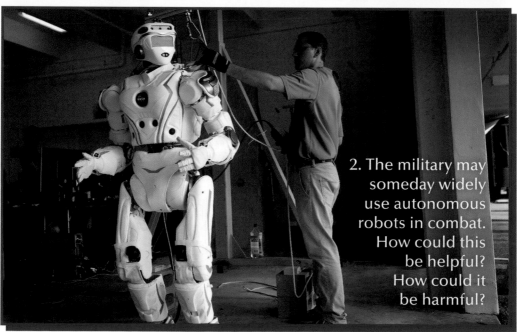

2. The military may someday widely use autonomous robots in combat. How could this be helpful? How could it be harmful?

3. Imagine you are sending a reconnaissance drone into enemy territory. What kinds of sensors do you think would be useful to gather information?

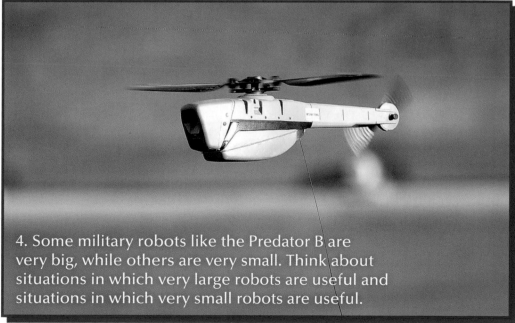

4. Some military robots like the Predator B are very big, while others are very small. Think about situations in which very large robots are useful and situations in which very small robots are useful.

GLOSSARY

autonomous: Undertaken or carried on without outside control.

civilian: A person not on active duty in the military.

deploy: To send something out to be used for a specific purpose.

ethics: Principles of conduct.

hazardous: Unsafe.

infrared: Referring to rays of light that people can't see and that are longer than rays that produce red light.

intelligence: Information gathered about enemies.

maneuver: To change position easily.

pandemic: An outbreak of disease that occurs over a wide geographic area and affects a great proportion of the population.

payload: The load carried by an aircraft or spacecraft.

radiation: Harmful waves of energy.

resistant: Opposing or preventing something.

satellite: A spacecraft placed in orbit around Earth, a moon, or a planet to collect information or for communication.

stealth: The act of doing something quietly and secretly.

surveillance: The act of watching someone or something closely.

virtual reality: An artificial environment that is experienced through sensory effects (such as sights and sounds) provided by a computer and in which one's actions partially determine what happens in the environment.

FIND OUT MORE

Books

Larson, Kirsten W. *Military Robots*. Mankato, MN: Amicus INK, 2018.

Martin, Brett S. *Military Robots*. Minneapolis, MN: Abdo Publishing, 2019.

Stark, William N. *Mighty Military Robots*. Mankato, MN: Capstone Press, 2016.

Websites

Drone Facts
www.softschools.com/facts/technology/drones_facts/3355/
This website offers a variety of fun facts about drones, including how they've been used in the military.

Drones to the Rescue
www.kidsdiscover.com/teacherresources/drones-uavs-rescue/
Check out these cool facts about drones and their amazing abilities.

Robot Facts for Kids
kids.kiddle.co/Robot
Learn all about robots on this fun and fact-filled website.

INDEX